Avenue of the Americas

Driving Green

Read My Lips

Three One-Act Comedies

by Martin Blank

American
Ensemble
Books

www.AmericanEnsembleBooks.Com

ISBN-13: 978-0-578-19891-0
Library of Congress Control Number: 2017919420

Published in the United States of America
FIRST EDITION

www.AmericanEnsembleBooks.Com

Contents

Avenue of the Americas

A Comedy in One Act

by Martin Blank

AVENUE OF THE AMERICAS was produced off-Broadway by Cantwell/Newsom Productions at the Tank Theater, premiering there on January 21, 2011. It was produced by Kristin Cantwell and Phil Newsome and directed by Katherine M. Carter. Lighting design was by Dan Jobbins, set design by Julia Noulin-Mérat, and sound design by Jillian Marie Walker. The stage manager was Griffin Parker.

The cast was as follows:

KATIE.............................. Laura Yost
JAY ....Timothy J. Cox
PHIL ....Chris Davis
THE MEN........................Leo Goodman
THE WOMEN .... Virginia Bartholomew

CHARACTERS:

KATIE, a woman in her late twenties or early thirties
JAY, a man in his forties
PHIL, a man in his late thirties
THE MEN, a man in his thirties
THE WOMEN, a woman in her thirties

TIME: A little while ago

SETTING: New Jersey and New York

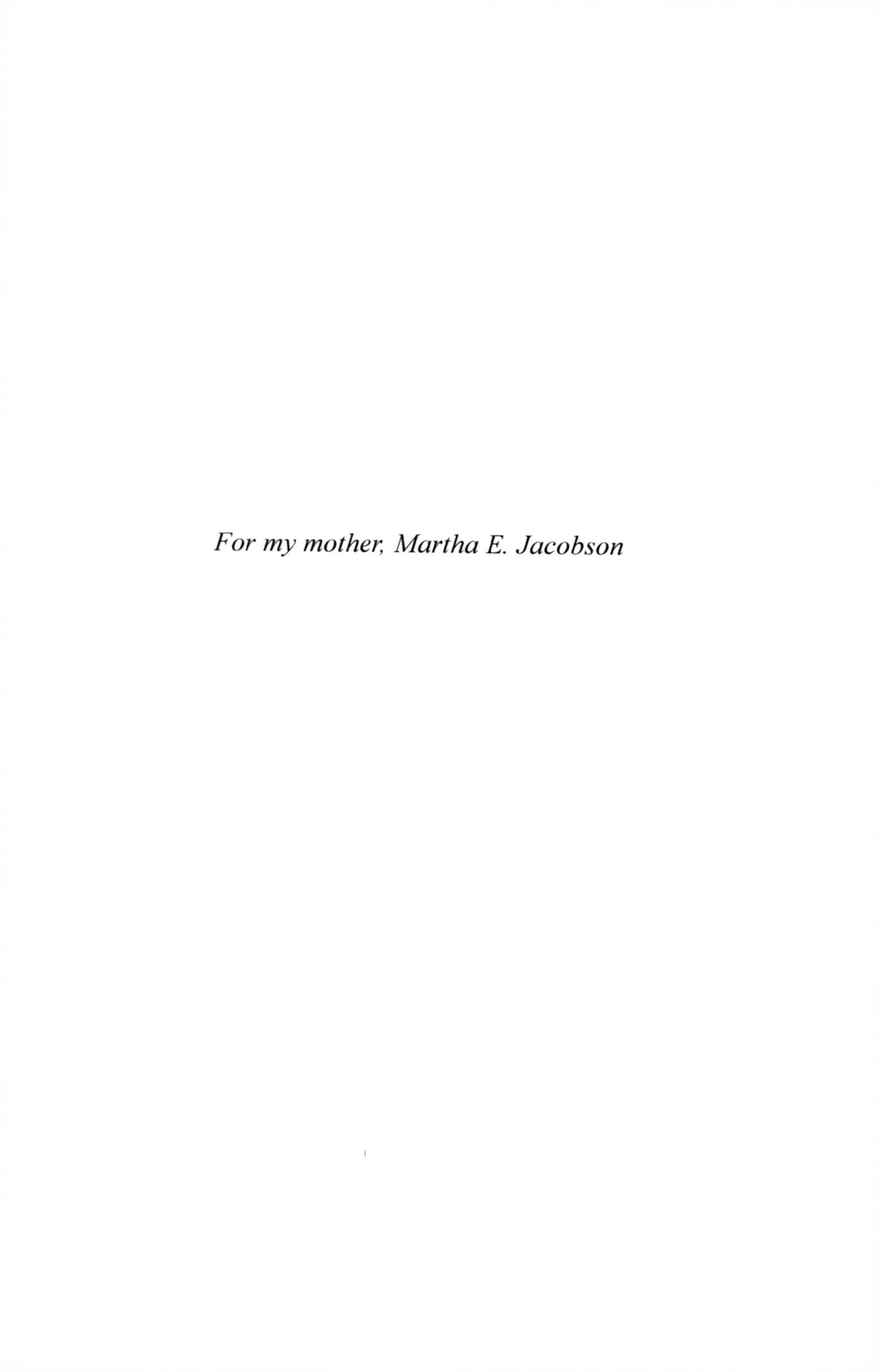

For my mother, Martha E. Jacobson

Lights up on Saint Mary's, a mental institution somewhere in New Jersey. Sitting in front of us is the single most beautiful girl in the world. Her name, Katie White, late twenties or early thirties, blonde, in sweater, skirt, and diamond earrings. She stares at a television. The flickering illumination lights her face. Drawings for storyboards of advertisements litter the floor. A moment, then she presses a remote. It sounds like we're in the middle of a soap. Organ music under offstage dialogue:

WOMAN (VOICE)

I didn't know that Bob had a twin!

MAN (VOICE)

It's true. Bob is dead. I'm the new Bob.

WOMAN

Your parents named you both Bob?

MAN

Yes. I mean no. I'm Frank, but I'm your new Bob.

WOMAN

I—I don't care, Bob-Frank. I love you anyway!

MAN

Erica, there's something very important I have to tell you.

WOMAN

Yes?

MAN

I just switched to GEICO and saved fifteen percent on car insurance!

(*Katie presses "mute" as an attendant enters.*)

KATIE

Know what's wrong with that ad?

ATTENDANT (GUS)

No.

KATIE

They only mentioned the product once.

GUS

Wouldn't know. Brought your *Ad Age.*

(*Katie takes magazine. Kisses Gus on the cheek.*)

Don't do that! Someone gonna see. Both be inna whole lotta trouble.

(*Katie speed-reads.*)

GUS

Katie, I know you don't mean nothing. Everyone knows Gus is a good Christian.

KATIE

Tonight on CBN, watch *The 700 Club.*

GUS

There's something important we got to talk about. Dr. Weinstein is dead.

KATIE

You told me.

GUS

So you gonna have a new doctor. Dr. Meyers. She might put you back in Wing B. I'm not allowed in B. This time might not be Wing B. This time, could be C.

(*Katie puts down magazine.*)

In C you in a room where you all alone. Just padding. No windows. Nothing. Sometimes they take you to another room and they shock you.

KATIE

Do they have TV?

GUS

No! No TV.

KATIE

No commercials?

GUS

No magazines. No nothing. Just terrible, horrible pain.

KATIE

Sounds like public TV.

(*Katie goes back to reading.*)

GUS (*grabbing her magazine)*
Meyers used to run C. No art supplies in C! You don't get to write no commercials.

KATIE
But I have an agency to run.

GUS
You don't!

KATIE
I spent several years with Earl, Leek, and Dunn.

GUS
You never did—

KATIE
Before that, I was with the Brown Group.

GUS
You never work those places!

KATIE
Yes, I have a resume.

GUS
You copied it out of some magazine!

KATIE

No!

GUS

Your name ain't White—it's Goldstein!

KATIE

Not true.

GUS

YOU BEEN HERE SINCE YOU WAS TEN!

(*silence*)

You want clothes from a catalog, who orders them for you? You want to run an ad agency. Who gets you art supplies? Books? Magazines? Why you want to leave Gus? (*pause*) If Meyers put you in C, Gus won't know you when you get out. You be dead inside. Who gonna teach Gus to read? Katie, I can't go to heaven unless I can read the Bible.

KATIE

You can read, Gus.

(*She gives Gus a magazine.*)

GUS

Do whatever Meyers says. Keep teaching ol' Gus how to read.

KATIE

Top, page sixty-nine.

GUS (*finding place*)

A new break thra . . . thra . . .

KATIE

Breakthrough . . . the word is "breakthrough."

GUS

Right. (*pause)* Coun-ter . . . counter ad-ver-tising.

KATIE

Gus.

GUS

Yes?

KATIE

You read just fine.

(*She kisses Gus on the cheek. Blackout.*)

Lights up on Dr. Meyers's office. Desk. Chair. A steel table with a device that's covered. Meyers has her hair up. Her glasses are small, wire-rimmed. She wears a gray dress covered by a shawl in an awful flower pattern. Katie tries to kiss Meyers on the cheek. Meyers recoils.

MEYERS

May I get you some coffee?

KATIE

A McCafé vanilla latte. It's like a giant vanilla unicorn just showed up to your mouth and wants to party.

MEYERS

Katie, Dr. Weinstein was with you for twenty years. That's highly unusual.

KATIE

Are you like me? I don't like singles bars. But then I found my soul mate on eHarmony dot com . . . .

MEYERS

Let's try something. Look at these and tell me what you see.

(*She shows Katie ink blots.*)

KATIE

Hey! McDonald's! (*sings*) Da da da-da. (*spoken*) I'm lovin' it!

(*next*)

Try new, improved Flintstones Chewables. Eat Wilma. Or Fred. How 'bout Barney?

(*next*)

Need extra work? Life getting to you? Join the National Guard.

MEYERS

All these remind you of advertisements. Why?

KATIE

Do you like my work? I could set up an account.

MEYERS

Account?

KATIE

For your advertising. What do you sell?

MEYERS

Nothing.

KATIE

Everyone sells something.

MEYERS

That's not true.

KATIE

Yes. Life equals sales. In bookstores now! Do you believe in Tiger Woods Syndrome?

MEYERS

(*a bad topic with Meyers*) Katie, we're not here to talk about Mr. Woods.

KATIE

The Tiger Woods Syndrome is a five-stage pattern a man uses to seduce a partner.

MEYERS

That's not the point.

KATIE

The Tiger Woods Syndrome marks an awakening. Shaky relationships are built on dishonesty. How about a relationship that is built on integrity?

MEYERS

Katie . . .

KATIE

You did buy the book?

MEYERS

Ah, no. No, Katie, I didn't. Listen, I'm going to come to the point. You're delusional. You think you're running an advertising agency.

KATIE

I am!

MEYERS

Dr. Weinstein allowed you to exist in a make-believe world. There are new and improved drugs that might help. I'd like to get you a teacher. You can study math, history, Greek . . .

KATIE

Little Caesars. A large Hot-N-Ready pizza . . . ready whenever you are. Little Caesars. Pizza. Pizza.

MEYERS

The first thing we're going to do is take away your art supplies.

KATIE

No!

MEYERS

Let me show you something.

(*She lifts cover from device.*)

I used it in Wing C. The latest model.

KATIE (*playing along*)

I could write a commercial for it!

(*Dr. Meyers places electrodes on Katie's head.*)

MEYERS

If I were to program at say . . . level one for three seconds . . . (*presses buttons*) you would feel some discomfort. Now I press "execute."

(*She does. Katie is uncomfortable.*)

If I were to program at say . . . level seven for five minutes, you would feel . . . pain. You might even pass out. But it won't kill you.

(*She takes out leather strap.*)

Of course, I would have to strap you in.

KATIE

When I was small, my mother would drink.

MEYERS

Good, very good, Katie. Tell me more.

(*Meyers puts down strap, takes electrodes off.*)

KATIE

We would have tea parties. I would drink tea. My mother, from a bottle. I would dress up. I had a flowered dress. The flowers were purple.

(*Katie gets up and begins to walk around. Meyers, pleased, takes a seat and writes notes on a pad.*)

MEYERS

Please. Tell me more.

KATIE

After tea, I would have to kiss my mother on the cheek.

(*Katie has circled behind Meyers. She kisses Meyers on the cheek and, like lightning, she grabs Meyers's shawl and uses it to tie Meyers to the chair.*)

MEYERS

What are you doing?!

KATIE

I have to go to New York.

(Katie crumples paper from note pad. She sticks it in Meyers's mouth, then swiftly uses leather strap on Meyers, attaches electrodes to Meyers's head, and programs machine.)

At level seven, for five minutes, you would feel . . . pain. You might even pass out. But it won't kill you.

(Meyers struggles violently!)

New Jersey Power . . . we'll turn you on!

(She kisses Meyers on the cheek. Hits button. Lights flicker to black.)

Lights up on an alley. Garbage cans. A streetlight casts stark shadows. We hear a Greyhound bus taking off into the distance. A HOOKER passes. Katie enters. A TOUGH crosses from behind trash can, moves toward Katie. Suddenly, he coughs.

KATIE

Billy? Why didn't you use NyQuil?

(Tough moves closer. Eyes Katie's purse and satchel. Scans the area one last time. He's about to make his move; Katie kisses him on the cheek. Tough pulls switchblade; it snaps open like a bullwhip.)

TOUGH (NICK)

You crazy? Never make a move like that.

(*silence*)

Hey, cut the silent treatment. Didn't mean to scare ya.

(*puts away blade, takes booze from coat*)

Stuff killed my folks. What the fuck?

(*takes swig, gives bottle to Katie*)

KATIE

What the fuck?

(*drinks*)

NICK

People call me Nick. Never seen ya round here.

KATIE

I'm going to New York City.

NICK

I work here. In Jersey. Someday I'm gonna be big . . . .
I'm gonna have a big house, and a family . . . and
an M-16 with a grenade launcher, like Pacino in
Scarface. . . .

KATIE

Scarface was a remake of the 1932 version staring Paul
Muni. Did you know one in every four movie dollars is
spent on pornographic films?

(*Nick considers this. He kisses Katie on the*

mouth. She likes it. The feeling is strange, new. Pause. Katie pulls away.)

You need Listerine.

NICK

Well, I know what you need.

(*Nick grabs her; this frightens Katie. She tries to pull away; he clutches her.*)

KATIE

No, no—I don't want to go to Wing C!

NICK

What?!

KATIE

Gus!

NICK

What the—

KATIE (*blood-curdling*)

GUS!!!!!!!!!!!!!!

NICK (*covering her mouth*)

What the fuck . . . ?

(*Katie tries to scream again. It comes out muffled. Our hooker rushes in and whacks Nick with her purse.*)

HOOKER (CINDY)

Leave her alone, you dick, you shit!

(Nick tosses Katie aside; things spill everywhere. He turns on Cindy, opens knife.)

NICK

And who are you? Catwoman?

(Cindy uses her purse to knock the blade out of Nick's hand. Hits him on the head with it. By the sound of it, there's something heavy in that purse. Nick's disoriented. Cindy knees him in the groin several times. He falls to the ground.)

CINDY

Had enough?

KATIE

Uh-oh . . . better call Maaco!

NICK

Has everyone gone fuckin' crazy?

(He gets the hell out. Cindy takes out a stick of gum, offers it to Katie.)

CINDY

Gum?

KATIE

Carefree.

CINDY

Yeah. Me too. Still, you need rules out here. Rule one: A man's dick is his weakness. Always exploit that. Rule two:

(*She takes a brick from her purse.*)

Carry insurance.

(*Cindy starts to gather Katie's things. Katie kisses Cindy on the cheek.*)

CINDY

It's okay.

(*sees Katie's artwork*)

This is really good. No kidding. Yours?

KATIE

Before I founded my own agency, I spent several years with Earl, Leek, and Dunn.

CINDY

I spent several years with Tom, Dick, and Harry.

KATIE

Are they in New York?

CINDY

They're everywhere. You got a name? No, I bet you have a card.

KATIE

Katie. Katie White.

CINDY

I'll grab ya a cab. Where you going?

KATIE

New York.

CINDY

You got a wad of cash?

KATIE

No.

CINDY

Well, you gotta have money to get to New York.

KATIE

That's what the man said.

CINDY

What man?

KATIE

At the bus station.

CINDY

You and that creep work together? You ain't tryin' ta con me, are ya? Tell you what. Those earrings . . .

(*She takes them.*)

Worth a ticket to New York City. Rule number three: If someone wants something . . . make them pay for it. Gonna put ya on the bus myself.

(*Blackout.*)

Lights up. A New York City street. People walk by. Traffic. A cab honks laughingly. Katie is by a pay phone. It rings. She picks it up.

KATIE (*into phone*)

Hello? Triple A? I need help!

(*Phil Scott, in his late thirties, worth beyond billions, stops dead at the sight of Katie. Since today is Tuesday, Phil is wearing the Rolex.*)

PHIL

Help? I'm at your service. Phil Scott. I've seen you before. The Manhattan Yacht Club?

KATIE

I write advertisements.

PHIL

For whom?

KATIE

Well, I want to write for the Jay Green Agency.

PHIL

Really? I know Jay. I'm heading uptown. Driver's off today. Why don't we share a cab?

(*Phil waves hand to hail a cab.*)

Lights up on four chairs. A cab. A long-haired teenage driver in a Guns N' Roses cap.

PHIL (*opening door*)

We'll go to Jay Green's office. I'll introduce you.

(*Katie jumps in cab.*)

DRIVER (ERIC)

Rock and roll!

PHIL

Take us to 40th and Madison, southwest corner. What's your name?

ERIC

Eric.

PHIL

Not you!

ERIC

Sorry, man. You look familiar.

PHIL

Yeah. Sometimes I'm in *Businessweek*.

KATIE

Philip W. Scott—grandson of Windsor. Chairman, CEO, the Windsor Scott Company. Defense, steel . . .

(*Eric turns on heavy metal music, bops to the beat.*)

. . . shipping!

(*Katie kisses Phil on the cheek. Blackout. Music continues.*)

Lights up on Jay Green's office. Jay is in his forties, an ex-Marine with a drinking problem. Presently, he drinks from a glass. Today is Tuesday: Jack Daniels.

JAY

We both know I've been trying to get Phil Scott's account for years.

KATIE

He uses Mike Walter Thompson.

JAY
I'd like to kill Mike, Walter, and Thompson.
(*hands Katie drink*)
Still, if I could only find Phil Scott's weakness . . .

KATIE
A man's dick is his weakness, Jay. Always exploit that.
(*Jay spits out drink. Katie downs hers.*)
Fuck it!

(*Jay pours himself another.*)

JAY
Right! Fuck it! Okay, enough chat. Let's see your stuff.

(*Jay unzips Katie's portfolio, looks at samples.*)

JAY
Where did you say you worked?

KATIE
Before I founded my own agency, I spent several years with Earl, Leek, and Dunn. Before that, I was with the Brown Group.

JAY (*perusing her resume*)
Right. You worked in New York. Did well. Set up your own shop in Jersey. Handled small clients I never heard of. Your stuff is strange, but strange can sell if it's original. Yours is. Your agency went belly up. Poor

management, I'm guessing. Now you want a job. Not a terribly new story.

KATIE

I write ads, Jay.

JAY

What's your philosophy?

KATIE

If someone wants something, make them pay for it.

JAY

Not bad.

(*shows Katie picture*)

My wife, Diana . . . my daughter, Tiffany. They are my philosophy. The reason this company exists is to make money. Money is the freedom to do other things . . .

(*points at picture*)

. . . for them. They are everything. What's important to you, Katie?

KATIE

Insurance.

JAY

Well, you haven't been offered a job yet.

KATIE

Always carry insurance.

JAY

Phil Scott brings you by the office. He's a big bull. I've wanted his account for years. What makes you think you can get it?

KATIE

I write ads.

JAY

Good. You're ballsy, but you know when to back off.

(*He downs drink.*)

Tell me this: what do you know about King Cosmetics?

KATIE

Martha King, queen of cosmetics, was born in Hilton Head. Her father, a millionaire, lost his fortune. Martha went to work as a teenager, selling cosmetics door to door. Years later, the Martha King Cosmetic Company was number one. However, in the last six months, King has plummeted to a distant second. King's main competitor is Beautycare. Insiders say . . .

(*Lights fade.*)

Lights up on Katie's new office. She is working at a fevered pitch. Martha King, one rich broad, enters. Martha looks to Katie, then:

MARTHA

Beautiful! They told me you like to keep busy. Hello. I'm . . .

KATIE

Martha King . . . of Martha King Cosmetics!

MARTHA

You are a vision. But you need makeup, honey. We all do.

(*Martha opens leather bag, skillfully begins to make Katie over.*)

KATIE

Did you know the average American male wants to look like Brad Pitt?

MARTHA

Men! Those Beautycare boys are so unsportsmanlike.

KATIE

The average American female wants—

MARTHA (*interrupting*)

When my quarterly report came out, those Beautycare boys actually sent me a dozen dead roses.

(*She holds mirror in front of Katie.*)

KATIE

Oh. I look like someone on TV.

MARTHA

No, you're too beautiful for TV. With your looks, you could be in the movies!

KATIE

Did you know one in every four movie dollars—

MARTHA

Never mind the agency talk. I've hired you, beautiful, to make King Cosmetics number one again.

KATIE

Research shows a shift in consumer behavior.

MARTHA

I know! A big sales contest.

KATIE

No. It's too late.

MARTHA

What—what do you mean?!

KATIE

You've lost your market share. Your only chance is to attack your opponent. Counter-advertising.

MARTHA

I'd be sued.

KATIE

If Beautycare does sue, it's free publicity. And if you use facts, it's tough to prove liability.

MARTHA

Well, I'd do anything to be on top again. Still . . .

KATIE

If your company goes bankrupt, it won't matter.

MARTHA

Bankrupt?!

KATIE

Or Martha King Cosmetics could be number one. See "Counter–Advertising," page sixty-nine.

MARTHA

Well, I would have to talk with my lawyers.

KATIE

Did you know the average American lawyer spends $942 a year on Xanax?

(*Blackout.*)

Lights up on a woman.

WOMAN

Let me tell you about me. I have a husband, two children. I own a home. I use Beautycare Cosmetics. Well I did . . . before the operation. One in five rats exposed to Beautycare Cosmetics got cancer. Me, I lost an arm. After the operation, my husband went to the drugstore to get my morphine. On the way, he plowed into a school bus, killing himself and forty-seven children. (*pause*) My two children were on that school bus. Now I'm alone. We had no insurance. What can a one-armed woman do for a living? Well, I won't be going back to my old job as a crossing guard. (*pause*) The bank is taking my house.

ANNOUNCER

Don't end up a one-armed, homeless morphine addict, with a dead husband and children. Use Martha King Cosmetics.

WOMAN

One of five rats exposed to Beautycare got cancer. Martha King. If I had only known.

(*Her plastic arm falls off. Lights fade.*)

Lights up on Katie's office, Katie hard at work. Phil enters with tray. On it, a pot of tea, Wedgwood cups and saucers.

PHIL

You take all your meals in your office. You won't return my calls.

KATIE

I live here.

PHIL

Why work all the time? If you could have anything, what would you want? If money were no object.

KATIE

Phil, I'd like a napkin.

(*He gives her one. Katie kisses Phil on the cheek.*)

PHIL

Me? I want to live forever. Guess I can't have that. (*pause*) My whole life, everyone wanted something from me. You don't. Why is that?

(*Katie works.*)

Katie? Would you like another napkin?

KATIE

Yes, please.

(He gives her one. Katie kisses Phil on the cheek.)

KATIE

I miss my dad.

PHIL

I miss my mother.

KATIE

My mother had a makeup table. Sometimes she would let me sit in front of it. She would brush my hair.

(pause)

PHIL

Katie? Would . . . would you like me to brush your hair?

(Katie nods. Katie takes brush from purse. Gives it to Phil. He tenderly brushes her hair.)

KATIE

Mommy . . . can I have a cookie?

PHIL

Later . . .

KATIE

I want one now.

PHIL

No.

(pause)

KATIE

Mommy, I want to watch TV.

PHIL

Okay, Katie. (*pause*) Would you like another napkin?

KATIE

Yes. Please.

(*Phil gives it to her. Katie softly kisses Phil on the mouth.*)

Fire and Ice by Trojan. You can't wait to get it on. Use of a condom may help prevent the spread of STDs.

PHIL

Let's get out of here.

KATIE

No. I don't want to leave!

PHIL

Okay. We can stay.

(*Phil turns off desk lamp. Darkness. Pause.*)

KATIE

Legs. Legs. Legs. (*laughs*) Fiddle Faddle. Head and

Shoulders. Sweet and Low. Banana. Banana. Tide?
Tide. Tide-Tide. Tide. Tide-Tide. Tide!

(*SCREAMS WITH MULTIPLE ORGASMS*)

TIDE FREE! REMOVES . . . MORE . . . RESIDUE
. . . FROM . . . DIRT . . . FOOD . . . AND STAINS!
TIDE FREE!!!!!!!!!!!

PHIL

Oh God.

KATIE

PALMOLIVE!

PHIL

Oh . . . my . . . God!

KATIE

PALMOLIVE!!

(*pause*)

Soft Scrub.

(*Sound of rain takes us to . . .*)

Jay's office. Lights up on Jay. Phil is with him. Jay drinks one after another.

JAY

It can't be this simple.

PHIL

Beautycare is going under. King's sales are up three hundred percent!

JAY

There's a catch!

PHIL

Catch? Katie was nominated for ten Clio Awards.

JAY

You want us to represent the Windsor Scott Company? No. You want something else . . .

PHIL

Make Katie co-owner.

JAY

You're fucking her . . . aren't you?

PHIL

Christ, Jay. This isn't *Speed-the-Plow*. This is real life.

JAY

I knew it. You're balling her.

PHIL

You had a partner before.

JAY

Twenty years ago. Harry was obsessed. Nearly killed the business. Harry had crazy ideas.
He thought advertising had a public duty, a responsibility. Oh, who cares? Phil, you inherited your success, I fought for mine.

PHIL

Still, I'm offering you the entire Windsor Scott account, defense, steel . . . and shipping.

JAY

And I should make Katie co-owner?

PHIL

Everyone knows the only big accounts you have are Martha King and Happy Cat.

JAY

Happy Cat is a money maker. Always has been. Always will be.

PHIL

Last year the Windsor Scott Group spent 900 million dollars on advertising. Want the account or not?

JAY (*picking up phone*)

Katie, get in here.

(*hangs up*)

I hope you're going to marry her.

PHIL

Well, I am thinking about it.

(*Blackout. A crash of THUNDER that would stir Shakespeare from his grave. Then church organ music.*)

Lights up on a priest.

PRIEST

I'd like to believe there's a higher power. But the big guy upstairs isn't going to protect us from those evil-doing, antichrist, terrorist bastards. Tough talk coming from a priest? Well . . . let's just say that during the Inquisition, if the Church had a Minuteman, or napalm, we would have used it.

(*Continues. He walks a few steps. Turns.*)

Right now . . . Allied Defense Systems is building a new weapons system. Called Smallpox. But Smallpox failed in test after test. One missile landed two hundred miles off-target, blowing up a Toys "R" Us in Cleveland. Fifty-seven little boys were in that Toys "R" Us. And twenty-two girls.

(*He moves toward us.*)

I want you to write your Congressman immediately and tell him . . . (*disapproving*) or her . . . that Allied Defense is the dark angel of a bottomless pit. You want the Windsor Scott Company to make Smallpox.

Windsor Scott just wants to build a few good weapons systems. Windsor Scott. They're heavenly.

(*Lights to black. Sounds of a crowd protesting.*)

Lights up on Katie's office. Jay falls in, his clothes torn. He drinks straight from a bottle.

JAY

I was attacked by a nun! (*pause*) She had me in a half nelson. I reversed the situation and got the sister in a sleeper hold. If I learned anything as a U.S. Marine, it's "kill or be killed."

KATIE

The few . . . the proud.

JAY

You're getting on my nerves, Katie. And we're messing with public opinion when the Church gets involved.

KATIE (holds up *Newsweek*, reading)

Counter-advertising! The big stick on the Madison Avenue playground. Katie White increased sales of Martha King Cosmetics—

JAY

I don't care what *Newsweek* said—

KATIE

Ms. White, co-owner of the Jay Green Agency—

JAY

You will tone down your ads! The one attacking Lively Feast cat food is going too far!

KATIE

The Happy Cat people are happy.

JAY

I don't care! We'll rewrite and reshoot that ad.

KATIE (*singing*)

Happy Cat. My cat is happy. Happy Cat!

JAY

This isn't a game!

KATIE

Gee. You sank my battleship!

JAY

Katie, who do you think you are?

KATIE

(*reads from* Newsweek)

Ms. White was not available for comment.

(*Jay throws bottle against wall.*)

JAY

Shut up. Are you going do what I say?!

KATIE

Jay . . .

JAY

What?!

KATIE

Better get the Bounty.

(*Blackout.*)

Lights on a little girl. She holds a dead cat—pets it.

GIRL

My cat is my best friend. This is Scruffy. Well, this was Scruffy.

(*drops cat with a loud thud*)

Scruffy is dead. How? Lively Feast cat food. There was a tin scrap in Scruffy's Seafood Delight. I saw blood squirt out of Scruffy's mouth. Now I'm in therapy. Lively Feast cat food was responsible for over ten thousand kitty deaths this year. That's more than choked on fur balls. Why? Because the people at Lively Feast don't care about your cat. Next time, buy Happy Cat cat food. Your parents, cat . . . and therapist will be happy you did!

(*picks up dead cat, skips off singing:*)

Happy Cat. My cat is happy. Happy Cat!

(*Blackout.*)

Lights up on Katie's office. As Katie moves around working, Phil follows.

PHIL

I want you to live with me.

KATIE

I live here, Phil.

PHIL

I don't understand why.

KATIE

First, I brainstorm for ideas.

PHIL

We've never been anywhere.

KATIE

Then I get more specific, but try to keep an open mind.

PHIL

You don't ask me for anything.

KATIE

Then I go to storyboard.

PHIL

Ask me for something.

KATIE

At some point, I have to narrow down the ideas. I try to hook the viewer. I ask myself, what would make the viewer pay attention?

PHIL

What do you want from me?

KATIE

I'm going to the Clio awards. I've been asked to give a speech.

PHIL

I'm not talking about an award. So you sell. My father sold. He worked so hard it sent him to the grave. There's more to life than sales. In a few years I turn forty. I think about death.

KATIE

Forest Lawn . . . it's a comfort to know they'll be there when it's time.

PHIL

Am I a joke to you?

KATIE

Once the storyboards are done, I have to get them approved by the client.

PHIL

Before you, my life was empty. Please—

KATIE

Approval can be a problem.

PHIL

I love you.

KATIE

One must always be ready and open to change.

PHIL

Katie White. You *are* an advertisement! You don't think. You don't feel. You can't love. But every tooth is white. Every hair is in place. You're perfect, but you're not real!

And I bought you . . . hook, line, and sinker.

KATIE

The Pocket Fisherman is back! Buy a Pocket Fisherman today!

(*Blackout.*)

Lights up. A New York City street. Night. A cab speeds by. Jay is with a detective who carries a leather satchel.

DETECTIVE (PETE)

Did I tell you—if you refer us to a divorce case, I'll find you a missing person for free?

JAY

I don't have time for this.

PETE

Would you like a free Frisbee?

JAY

What did you find out?

PETE (*taking file from satchel*)

Her real name isn't White. It's Goldstein. Yeah, Katie Goldstein. She escaped from Saint Mary's . . . a mental institution in Jersey.

(*Pete hands file to Jay.*)

JAY (*removing picture*)

Katie Goldstein. Jesus. Her father Harry was my partner twenty years ago. I have to go.

PETE

Would you like a free T-shirt?

JAY

Hey, you don't know me. We never met.

(*Blackout*.)

Lights up on Katie's office as Jay enters.

JAY

I just got off the phone. Windsor Scott dropped their account. And Happy Cat is switching to Mike Walter Thompson.

KATIE

Out of work? Have you thought of a job in computer programming?

JAY

Katie Goldstein . . . Who do you think I am?

KATIE

Nice guy. Too bad about the dandruff.

JAY

You're like your father. My God, you have put truth in advertising.

KATIE

I'm co-owner, Jay!

JAY

This isn't a game.

KATIE

Can we play again?

JAY

We have a handful of small clients left. We could go under.

KATIE

(*not unkindly*) Poor management, I'm guessing.

JAY

Okay. It's not my fault your father was a nervous man. Leave now. I'm not asking.

(*Lights fade, then up on four chairs. A car. Katie's mother and father sit in the front two seats. Katie's mom has had too much to drink. Katie crosses to them, sits in back.*)

MOTHER

I'm not asking.

FATHER

I have my award.

(*holds up crumpled brown paper*)

I have my speech.

MOTHER

Harry, you're nothing but a small, weak man. You wrote that speech on the side of a shopping bag.

KATIE (*age ten*)

Mommy?

MOTHER (*drunk*)

Katie, shut up.

FATHER

Don't talk to her like that!

MOTHER

Everyone tonight will know Jay Green pushed you out. If you had any guts, you'd walk up to Jay and punch him in the face. I hear Green's wife won't sleep with him unless he has a good year.

FATHER

Not in front—

MOTHER (*grabs his speech*)

Pathetic!

FATHER

Give it back.

KATIE (*grabs speech*)

I got it, Daddy.

MOTHER

Katie! Give it to me!

FATHER

Stop. Don't hit her!

(*turns*)

Katie, do what your mother says.

KATIE

DADDY!!!!!!!!!!!!!

(*Blackout. Sound of a car crash. Ambulance. A little girl starts to cry.*)

Lights up on Katie, age ten, with Dr. Weinstein at Saint Mary's. Katie clutches the brown piece of paper.

DR. WEINSTEIN

Hello, Katie. I'm Dr. Weinstein. Don't you want to say hello? Can I see what you're holding?

(*Katie puts paper down her dress.*)

DR. WEINSTEIN

Katie, if you don't want to show me, that's alright. You're a very pretty little girl. Would you like to watch TV?

(*Katie nods. Blackout. Sound of rain.*)

Lights up on Jay and Katie.

JAY

What's your decision?

(*Katie pulls a very old crumbled piece of brown paper from under her dress.*)

KATIE

The Clio Awards. I'm going to give my father's speech.

(*Blackout. Christmas music.*)

Lights up. Jay's office.

JAY (*on phone*)

Diana, why are you leaving me? Say that again! What do you mean Tiffany doesn't want to talk to me? Diana, listen—it's Christmas. I'm alone. All my clients have dropped their accounts. Hello? Hello?!

(*A gun dealer enters. Jay slams down phone.*)

You're late!

GUN DEALER (JIMMY)

What do I look like? Stop and Shop?

(*He throws gun on Jay's desk. Jay throws cash at Jimmy.*)

JAY

Hold on. I need bullets.

JIMMY

Not smart for a man in my line to carry ammo.

JAY

It's Christmas. I'm in a hurry. Fix it.

JIMMY

You're the smart ad exec. Check the Yellow Pages.

JAY

Let my fingers do the walking.

(*Jay rifles though Yellow Pages.*)

JIMMY

It's Christmas. Why the hurry?

JAY

I have to kill someone.

JIMMY

I didn't hear that, pal. And you'll get caught. Better wait 'till you're sober.

JAY (*pointing*)

Murray's Guns. Guns and ammo. 1251 Avenue of the Americas. Open twenty-four hours, 365 days a year! You! Get out!

JIMMY

Yeah . . . a merry fucking Christmas to you too.

(*Lights fade.*)

Single shaft of light on Katie. Sound of rain, then applause. Katie is wet, beautiful. A fashion model enters, smiles, waves to audience for all it's worth, then hands Katie award.

KATIE (*reading from brown paper*)

Gentlemen, advertising, as we practice it, is altering consumer behavior. Fine. We want to sell products.

(*Sound of wind. Angry. Strobe light. Jay enters in black ski mask.*)

But . . . we are seducing our children. Future generations will be bored . . . anxious. Unable to connect with others. They will crave material things, yet find their purchase an empty, hollow experience.

(*Jay points gun at Katie.*)

But it's not too late. There are simple steps we can take. One, as the British do, cluster commercials every thirty minutes.

(*The model sees gun—runs toward Jay.*)
Two, make ads honest by selling facts about a product, not an image.
(*Katie looks at gun. She has no fear.*)
Three, advertisements targeted at children . . .

(*The model is too late. Six shots. Each loud. Deadly. Katie falls to the ground dead, still a beautiful dream. Blackout.*)

Lights up on Jay sitting quietly in front of a TV, which, for now, is silent. A year later. Jay looks tired, stares blankly. After all, Jay is at Saint Mary's, a mental institution somewhere in New Jersey. Gus enters.

GUS
It's me, Gus. Don't you have anything to say? Some day you gotta say something. Lord, have mercy.

(*He turns up TV volume, leaves. It sounds like we're in the middle of a soap. Organ music under prerecorded dialogue:*)

WOMAN (VOICE)
I didn't know that Bob had a twin!

MAN (VOICE)
It's true. Bob is dead. I'm the new Bob.

WOMAN

Your parents named you both Bob?

MAN

Yes. I mean no. I'm Frank, but I'm your new Bob.

WOMAN

I—I don't care, Bob-Frank. I love you anyway!

MAN

Erica, there's something very important I have to tell you.

WOMAN

Yes?

MAN

I just switched to GEICO and saved fifteen percent on car insurance!

(*Jay turns off the set, stares at us, mad as a loon.*)

JAY

They only mentioned the product once.

(*Blackout.*)

END OF PLAY

Driving Green

A Ten-Minute Comedy

by Martin Blank

DRIVING GREEN

DRIVING GREEN was first produced by Journeymen Theater Ensemble (Krista Cowan, Interim Artistic Director; Andrew Wassenich, Producing Director) in Washington, D.C., premiering on July 10, 2009. It was directed by David E. Binet, the lighting design was by Chris Holland, and the stage manager was Shanice L. Jones.

The cast was as follows:

TOM . . . . Slice Hicks
BETH . . . . Jill Levin
DALE . . . . Matt Dewberry

CHARACTERS:

TOM, 30s
BETH, 30s
DALE, a man or woman, any age

TIME: Now

SETTING: Car suggested by two chairs and a steering wheel/dashboard

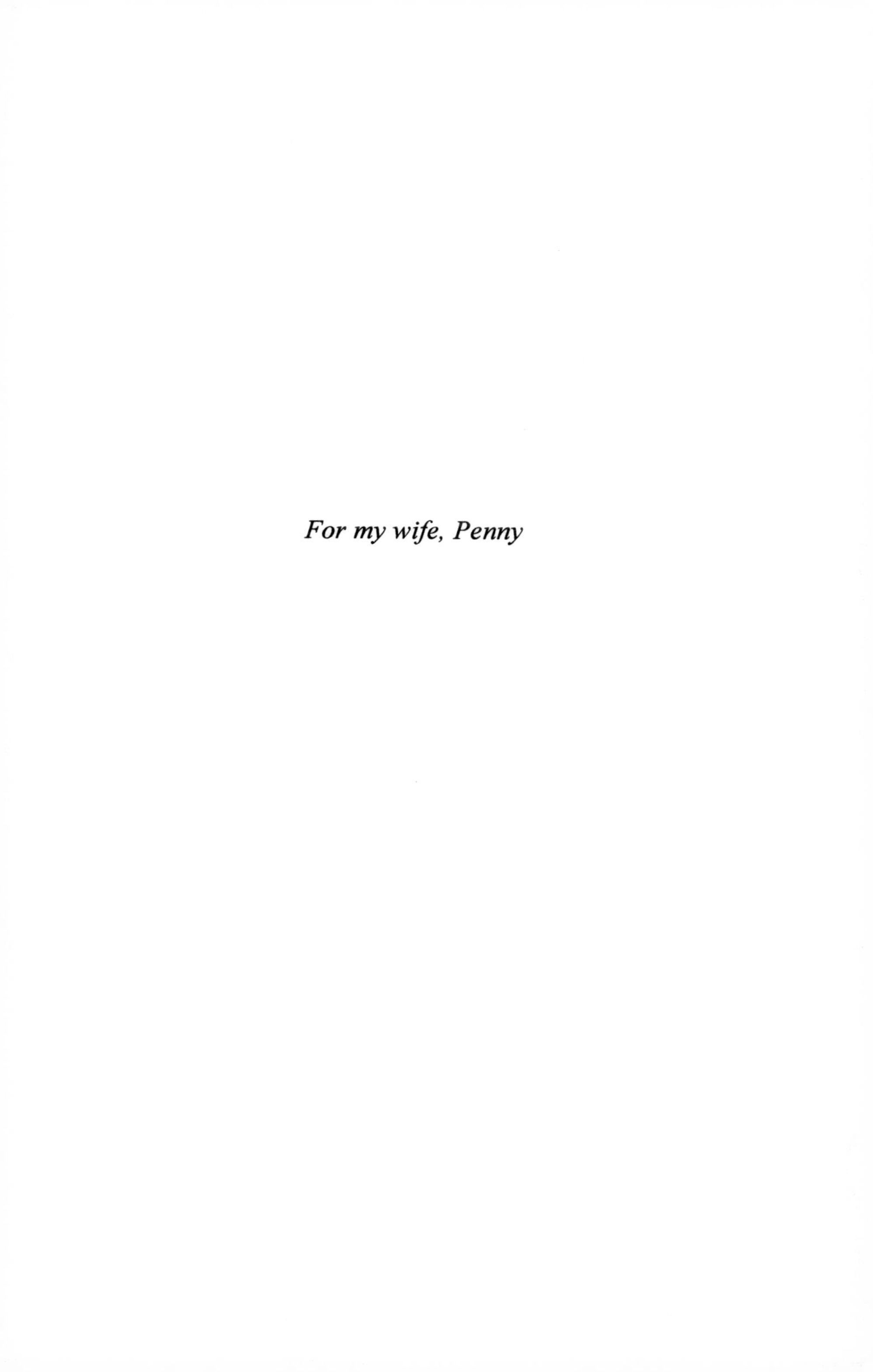

For my wife, Penny

(Lights up on married couple in a car suggested by two chairs and a steering wheel/dashboard. TOM, in driver's seat, wipes sweat from his forehead. BETH is immersed in the Washington Post.*)*

TOM

This car is an oven. I'm burning up.

BETH

The windows are open.

TOM

I want to roll up them up. Turn on the—

BETH (*taking out calculator*)

Do you know what turning on the air conditioning would do to our carbon footprint?

TOM

I'm late for work every day because you insist on this sado-masochistic ride-sharing. When I'm late to work—yet again—I'll have to park blocks from work. I hate this hybrid. It cramps my legs.

BETH

A small price for driving green.

TOM

If anyone at work sees me in this car—

BETH

So, resign.

TOM

Quit NAP?

BETH

The National Association of Petroleum is destroying our planet. How do you sleep at night?

TOM

We don't just sleep . . .

BETH (*smiles*)

No. We don't.

TOM

Come on, traffic, move! Move!

BETH

Face it. We're not going anywhere.

TOM

I'm burning up.

BETH

It's global warming.

TOM (*mocking*)

Global warming is a fact?

BETH

Even you must know the PR you put out is delusional.

TOM

Delusional? Yeah? Well, the people in your office are insane.

BETH

My associates are liberals.

TOM

They're stoned.

BETH

The men at NAP drink and go around with hookers.

TOM

We don't all drink.

BETH

You go around with hookers, then?

TOM

Of course not. I love you. Even if your shoes are made from recycled tires.

BETH

At least my feet aren't covered in dead cow.

TOM

I see. Rethinking our marriage?

BETH

I'm sure it's not worth talking about.

TOM

Not worth talking about?

BETH

I guess I could say something about the mail.

TOM

The mail?

BETH

Yes, the mail. I've tried to get us paperless. What mail does come, you never put in the same place twice. It could be anywhere. It's like an Easter egg hunt. I hate it when you get the mail before me. I have a system. Three categories: read now, read later, recycle now. With you, the important stuff gets lost. The junk stays around until Earth Day. Also, you write people letters, thereby killing trees. As well as the fossil fuel to transport it. Thus emitting greenhouse gases, unless, fingers crossed, the mail truck runs on hydrogen. And I've actually seen you drive three blocks to the mailbox. Would it kill you to walk?

TOM

No. The mail. Is that it? I mean, don't you disdain my job and everything it represents? I work for the sole purpose of accumulating material things. Your freegan pals are right in that my job is stressful, boring, and monotonous—unless, of course, a guy comes to work with a really good hooker story.

BETH

You are right to say some freegans oppose working more hours than necessary to survive.

TOM

Great. Rationalized laziness.

BETH

To save the planet, you have to start somewhere. The mail was as good a place as any.

TOM (*disingenuous*)

Then there is global warming to consider.

BETH

Goes without saying.

TOM

What about you?

BETH

Me?

TOM

Yes, you and your limousine liberal vegan friends, who preach tolerance but won't tolerate an opinion other than their own. Trust fund twits bragging about investing in socially conscious mutual funds when they own stock in Exxon Mobil, buying green houses and driving sport utility vehicles. Balding husbands in painted tans, with multiple facelifts. Their wives drinking spinach smoothies, sitting around solar-heated swimming pools, with silicon breast implants, a non-biodegradable product made by Dow Chemical, the company that brought you napalm. With vegetarian teenage children sneaking McDonalds cheeseburgers, collecting money for Greenpeace, secretly hoping it will get them into Vassar. The family sitting around the dinner table eating pumpernickel bread, carrots, and turnips they found while dumpster diving, droning on about T. Boone Pickens and his plan. I say screw 'em. I want my meat cooked on a charcoal grill, rare. I want to drive a '60s muscle car and, when I floor it, I can see the needle on the fuel gauge go down, down, down. I say live and live now. Because there's a good chance some crazy we pissed off at Gitmo is going to get his hands on a biological weapon or a dirty nuke and use it.

BETH

OK, some of the people we know are hypocrites, but many, many—let me finish—are not. What happened to doing the right thing? I know I can't control some fanatical group waving a giant mushroom cloud flag. I'm one person. So are you. And we can hope to make a difference. Do something everyday. Even if it's sharing a ride in a hybrid car. Or paying bills online. If you've lost all hope, who are you and what have you done with the beautiful man I met in AmeriCorps?

TOM

You really want to try to stop so-called global warming?

BETH

It's real. And I do.

TOM

Then we both know—

BETH

Don't you dare say it.

TOM

Wind, solar, bio are a start . . .

BETH

You'll regret it!

TOM

If you can't stomach the truth . . .

BETH

The truth? The truth is I'm hot! I wish you could turn on the air conditioning.

TOM

Maybe I will.

BETH

Shut up. Fine. You win, turn on the AC. Just don't say—

TOM

No, I'm gonna leave the windows open. So the entire world can hear.

BETH

Don't do it.

TOM

If global warming is real, and if it can be stopped . . .

BETH

I'll put on the radio really, really loud.

TOM

The radio uses power. What about our carbon footprint?

BETH

Drat!

TOM

If you want to save Mother Earth . . .

BETH

Please.

TOM

The only way to fully drive green is . . .

BETH

Don't say it!

TOM

. . . nuclear power.

(*Beth pounds Tom's head on dash/steering wheel—with next five words.*)

BETH

Never. Say. Those. Words. Again.

(*Pause, Tom tries to recover.*)

TOM

I think you cracked the GPS.

(*DALE, in a blue blazer, enters.*)

DALE

Excuse me. There were several loud, violent noises. Is everything okay?

TOM

Fine.

BETH

Fine, thank you.

DALE

Perhaps you'd like to take the Prius off the showroom floor for a test drive?

TOM

Oh, no. We're doing our test now.

BETH

To see if it stands up to our morning routine.

DALE

Well, when you get the car on the road . . .

TOM

Look, can you give us a moment?

DALE

(*sensing a sale, quickly leaves*)

Certainly. I'll be at my desk when you need me.

(*Tom and Beth are now alone.*)

BETH

Energy waster!

TOM

You know what you can do with your carbon calculator?

BETH	TOM
I want a divorce!	I want a divorce!

(*Pause. Stony silence. Then, both smile.*)

BETH
I don't really.

TOM
I don't really.

BETH
Shall we buy the car?

(*They kiss. Blackout.*)

END OF PLAY

Read My Lips

A Comedy in One Act with Dance

by Martin Blank

READ MY LIPS

READ MY LIPS was first produced by NewGate Theatre, Providence, Rhode Island. It premiered there on September 7, 1994, with David Tulli, producing director. It was directed by Brien Lang and choreographed by Deb McGowan.

MIKE . . . . Jim O'Brien
SANDY. . . . . Lisa Vecchione
FRANCES. . . . . Clare Vadeboncoeur
DR. NANCY CHANG . . . . .Christine Byrnes
MIKE'S SHADOW . . . . .Ed DeBoo
SANDY'S SHADOW. . . . . .Deb McGowan
DR. NANCY CHANG'S SHADOW . . . . A. Vainus

CAST 5W, 2M

MIKE, 20s
SANDY, 20s
FRANCES, 60s
DR. NANCY CHANG, 30s

(Each character has another actor playing their Shadow, except Frances, who is quite dead.)

TIME: Now

SETTING: Los Angeles

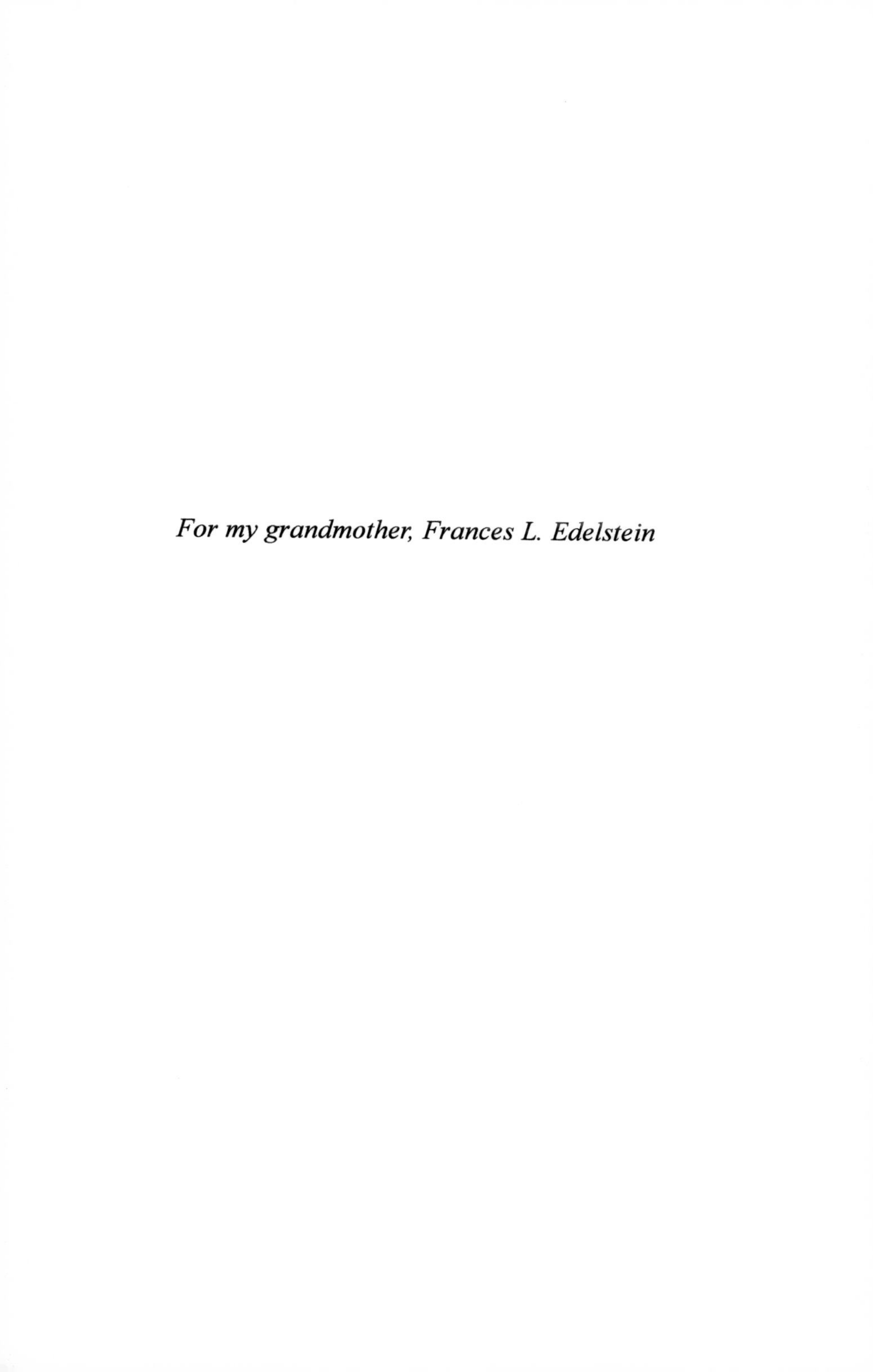

For my grandmother, Frances L. Edelstein

PRE-SHOW

Upstage, a cemetery. The sound of wind.

Before curtain, Frances, pale-faced, wanders through the theater.

She carries a basket of cookies. She silently offers cookies to any takers.

The effect is eerie.

FADE TO BLACK.

SHOW

Lights on Frances in the cemetery. She starts out with a look that would scare George S. Patton.

FRANCES

The cookies contain poison!

A smile.

FRANCES (cont.)

Just a little humor from the hereafter. The cookies are fine. In fact, they're kosher. I'm Frances Lipman. This is a story about my son, Michael.

Michael, late 20s, enters, kneels.

FRANCES (cont.)

It is a sin for a Jew not to visit the grave of a parent once a year. It's taken my son five years. What is it that made my son stay away so long? And what is it that finally made him come?

Music.

Frances walks off. Mike remains. He tries to go. But a group of dancers with flashlights moves, throwing beams of light on Mike. The dancers block his every attempt to leave.

Music cross-fades with the sound of a helicopter. The chopper gets closer.

It passes, loud and fast.

It scares the dancers. They run off, taking Mike with them.

Frances enters the cemetery. At the same time, Sandy enters CENTER, wearing a bright leotard. Sandy "freezes" in position.

FRANCES

This is Michael's girlfriend, Sandy. It was exactly five years ago when they first met.

Sound of two people walking up steps. A door is opened, closed.

Mike enters in a bright leotard. Sandy "unfreezes."

SANDY

Nice apartment.

MIKE

West L.A. stucco.

SANDY

It's strange, though?

MIKE

Strange?

SANDY

Living over a sex shop.

MIKE

They sell underwear.

SANDY

Chains, leather, whips . . .

MIKE

The S&M are really a very discreet group. That's what I've been told—by the store's owner. Did you know they have an annual convention in Cleveland?

SANDY

You're kidding.

MIKE

No. Every year the sadists vote to move the convention to Los Angeles, but every year the masochists keep choosing Cleveland.

Sandy smiles.

MIKE

Would you like something?

SANDY

Tea, if you have it?

MIKE

I have.

Mike crosses to a small table, makes tea. Mike's Shadow enters and dances to Sandy—who cannot hear what Mike's Shadow says.

SANDY

Tell me another Hollywood story.

MIKE'S SHADOW

(to Mike as he dances around Sandy) She's very pretty. I mean, she's very beautiful. And bright. All Mother would ask for . . . is she Jewish?

MIKE

So. The Marx Brothers. Chico Marx had a reputation for being vulgar with women. Chico is at a party. A young, new star, Tallulah Bankhead, enters. Chico goes straight for her. The room falls silent. But to everyone's surprise, Chico is a complete gentleman. The two exchange pleasantries, then Chico says, I'd really like to fuck you. Bankhead replies, so you shall, you old-fashioned boy.

SANDY

Where do you get your endless supply of Hollywood stories?

MIKE

My mother and father wrote about film for the *L.A. Times*.

SANDY

I'd love to meet them.

MIKE

You can't.

SANDY

Why?

MIKE

They're dead.

SANDY

I'm sorry. I mean, I don't know anything about you, other than you live above the Pleasure Chest, and you tell wonderful Hollywood stories.

MIKE

What do you want to know?

SANDY

Tell me about your work.

MIKE

Public relations. It would bore you.

SANDY

No, what . . . what are you working on now?

MIKE

It's not interesting.

SANDY

Mike, I'm sure it's interesting.

MIKE

Bread crumbs.

SANDY

Bread crumbs?

MIKE

Bread crumbs.

SANDY

I read something about bread crumbs in the paper.

MIKE

Right. How do you get bread crumbs into the *L.A. Times*?

SANDY

Who would want to?

MIKE

The Bread Crumb Institute.

SANDY

They have an institute?

MIKE

Sure, I also represent wheat, and eye disease. *(pause)* I'm really just starting.

SANDY

What do you do . . . for these institutes?

MIKE'S SHADOW

Overbill them.

MIKE

Get them in the news. *(spills tea)* Oy . . . that's hot.

SANDY

You're Jewish?

MIKE

So . . .

SANDY

You don't look it—not at all.

MIKE

I took a class at UCLA. JEW101. On the eighth day, they circumcise you. Then you spend the rest of the semester arguing.

SANDY

I'm Jewish.

MIKE

I know.

SANDY

How can you tell?

MIKE'S SHADOW

(dances) Do the words "nose job" mean anything? If you ate with a plastic fork, it would be cannibalism!

MIKE

I don't know. I just can.

SANDY

When did you start ballet?

MIKE

Ten months ago, when my mother . . . well, like I said—I don't want to discuss it.

SANDY

You have to go to the cemetery soon.

MIKE

I know. Can we talk about something else?

SANDY

Okay. *(pause)* Why did you pick me up?

MIKE

What are you talking about?

SANDY

Come on. You picked me up!

Mike's Shadow lifts Sandy in the air.

MIKE

You let me.

SANDY

(meekly holds out cup) More tea?

MIKE'S SHADOW

Tell her a Hollywood story.

MIKE

(takes cup, gets more tea) Would you like to hear another Hollywood story?

SANDY/SANDY'S SHADOW

Yes!

MIKE

Dorothy Parker, poet, critic, screenwriter, was famous . . .

SANDY

Why did you stop?

MIKE

The look on your face.

Mike brushes Sandy's cheek.

SANDY

Go on. I want you to kiss me.

They kiss.

A helicopter passes by. They hold each other close.

Mike and Sandy's Shadows take CENTER. Lights shift.

Music: the tango! Mike and Sandy's Shadows tango.

Music out. They stop.

MIKE'S SHADOW

Dorothy Parker, poet, critic, screenwriter, was famous for her many quips. A loud woman at a party noticed a soldier and turned to Dorothy, "It's his uniform. I just love soldiers." Replied Parker, "Yes, you have in every war."

Music. Shadows tango. Music stops. They stop.

MIKE'S SHADOW

What most people don't know about Dorothy Parker is she had an affair with playwright Charles MacArthur, which left her pregnant. She had an abortion, which left her devastated.

Music. Shadows tango. Music stops. They stop.

MIKE'S SHADOW

After the abortion, Dorothy Parker ran from life. Attempted suicide. In fact, she tried it more than once. The second time, Robert Benchley visited her at the hospital. He said, "Dottie . . . if you don't stop this sort of thing, you'll make yourself sick."

Tango music. Music stops. They stop.

SANDY'S SHADOW

Fall in love with me.

MIKE'S SHADOW

I already have.

Music. They tango off. Frances enters.

FRANCES

One year fades into another. Winter, spring, summer, fall—they become a blur. Five years pass. Mike lives with Sandy.

Frances exits.

An L.A. sunrise.

Music.

Sandy's Shadow enters, kneels, holding out arms, becoming a treadmill. Mike walks in place.

Sandy enters, dances to Mike. Mike and Sandy fight, but we can't hear them over the chopper.

Music cross-fades with loud helicopter. Mike's Shadow is missing.

SANDY

I want the police in the street, not the air.

MIKE

You're changing the subject!

SANDY

I'm not.

SANDY'S SHADOW

You are.

MIKE

Where do you want to go to dinner? Clyde's or Red Lobster?

SANDY

Either is fine.

SANDY'S SHADOW

Red Lobster.

MIKE

Clyde's or Red Lobster?

SANDY

It doesn't matter.

SANDY'S SHADOW

Red Lobster!

MIKE

Will you make a decision!

SANDY

Read my lips: I don't care!

SANDY'S SHADOW

Red Lobster ! Red Lobster ! I . . . WANT . . . TO . . . GO . . . TO . . . RED LOBSTER!!!

MIKE

We'll go to Clyde's.

SANDY

Clyde's is fine.

MIKE

Certain?

SANDY

I am. *(beat)* Michael, darling. When was the last time we went out to do something fun? Other than eat out. You know, F.U.N.?

MIKE

Fun? Like attending that lunch with your fellow philosophy majors? I sat next to one of your classmates . . .

SANDY

Please don't start in on Alvin!

MIKE

Alvin is the most boring guy I've met in my entire thirty years of life. From now on, I'll simply refer to him as "Laughing Boy." He spent TWO hours trying to convince me I didn't exist. If I could only have convinced him he didn't exist . . .

SANDY

When was the last time we went to a movie—or you told me a Hollywood story? What are you running from?

MIKE

I'm not running.

SANDY

What about the cemetery?

MIKE

Why do you always bring that up?

SANDY'S SHADOW

It's your weakness. Weakness. Weak—

SANDY

Ever since you were on the cover of *L.A. Magazine* . . . all you do is work. Defense, nuclear plants, my God, you're working for the tobacco industry.

MIKE

Such as it is. Business is business, Sandy.

SANDY

You've become a public relations whore!

MIKE

(gets off treadmill) Me? A whore? What about you? Hiding out from life at the university. You donate money to some museum so you can go to an art opening, where some guy has painted a canvas white. The artist cries out, "Love, I want all of you to see love." Meanwhile . . . the guy's got the clap.

Sandy starts to go.

MIKE

Sandy, stop! I feel kinda sick. What . . . what do you want?

Mike and Sandy's Shadows dance off.

SANDY

I don't want you to leave me.

Sound of helicopter fades in.

MIKE

I'm not going to . . .

SANDY

Are you sure? I'm here, fighting for our relationship. And I can't do it alone.

Mike has a funny look.

MIKE

I need to lie down, Sandy. Can we talk about this later?

SANDY

Haven't you been listening to me?! *(pause)* I'm sorry. You . . . you do look pale. Are you okay?

MIKE

(forced smile) I'm fine. I just need to nap.

Blackout. Music that reminds us of a doctor's office.

Something like the soundtrack from Psycho . . . or Vertigo!

Lights on a part of the stage probably not used before.

This is Dr. Chang's office.

At minimum, there might be an anatomy of the human body on the wall. Maybe an examining table as well.

A Shadow in death mask with a screen door dances on. Mike opens the door and goes through, as two black chairs are danced on. Mike sits. Mike's Shadow stands.

Dr. Chang dances on.

DR. CHANG

Luckily for you, I do internal medicine as well as gastroenterology.

MIKE

That's impressive.

DR. CHANG

No big deal.

DR. CHANG'S SHADOW

It's very impressive.

MIKE

Before we begin, there's something I have to tell you.

DR. CHANG

Take your time.

DR. CHANG'S SHADOW

Hurry. I must be at the cleaners in five minutes.

MIKE

Since my mother died—for the last few years, that is—I've had some . . . well . . . a lot of anxiety over any medical problem. So, I'll be okay. But you have to go slow.

DR. CHANG

Oh, Michael. I had a woman come in here last week.

She had a little pain right here. A little pain. It turned out to be a tumor. I think she's gonna die. She's 32. And we ask . . . how is this possible? Are you okay, Michael?

MIKE'S SHADOW

I'm going to die.

MIKE

I'm fine.

DR. CHANG

Not to worry. Dr. Chang is on the case.

DR. CHANG'S SHADOW

What does "previously owned Mercedes" mean, anyway? Any other car is called a used car. I should have bought new.

DR. CHANG

What seems to be the problem?

MIKE

I have pain, here.

DR. CHANG

Any other symptoms?

MIKE

No, just stomach pain.

DR. CHANG

On a one-to-ten scale?

MIKE

A six. Seven. I—

DR. CHANG

Quiet for a moment, please.

Chang listens to Mike's stomach with her stethoscope. Chang's Shadow listens to Chang with her stethoscope.

DR. CHANG'S SHADOW

Also, the leather in the back seat is beginning to crack.

MIKE

Is something wrong?

DR. CHANG

Just doing my job. I saw you on the cover of *L.A. Magazine*.

MIKE

Business has tripled.

Chang pokes Mike's stomach. Chang's Shadow pokes Chang.

DR. CHANG

This hurt?

MIKE

No.

DR. CHANG

Here.

MIKE

Yes. A seven.

DR. CHANG

Good. Well, not good. But . . . *(takes Mike's blood pressure)* . . . you seem tired, Michael.

MIKE

I've been working late.

DR. CHANG

But your blood work was normal. Your blood pressure is a little high, but I'd say your other vital signs are very good. Have you been nervous?

MIKE

Deadlines, yes . . .

CHANG

From the sound of your stomach, I think all you have is gas.

MIKE

Gas?

DR. CHANG

Here are some samples. Use as directed. What you need is to take it easy. Rest. Eat mild foods for a while. Jell-O. Soup.

MIKE

So there's nothing wrong.

DR. CHANG

I think you're gonna be fine.

MIKE

I'm gonna be fine?

DR. CHANG'S SHADOW

How should I know? I wonder what a tune-up would cost?

MIKE

I'll be okay?

DR. CHANG

I think so.

Helicopter. Lights on Frances.

FRANCES

If I taught Michael anything, it was to work hard. My son did, for a very long time. Success did not come in small pieces for Michael. Unfortunately, it came all at once.

Lights on apartment. Sandy's Shadow is missing.

SANDY
Are you moving to Washington, D.C., or not?

MIKE
It's a chance to work for a U.S. Congressman. How many people does that happen to?

SANDY
It would seem, far too many.

MIKE
Come to Washington with me.

SANDY
You know I won't run. I have a year left on my Ph.D.

MIKE
Sandy, sometimes you have to run.

SANDY
I've never run from anything in my life. When I was in Girl Scouts, I hated it. I could never pitch a tent, or light a fire. Well, I did manage to set a tent on fire.

MIKE
You're making this up.

SANDY

No, this is real life. The point is, I hated it, and I didn't quit. I was always taught that things worthwhile take hard work and sacrifice.

MIKE

D.C. is a plane ride away.

SANDY

I . . . won't just let you leave me. Remember the time we were walking late one night on Sunset Boulevard? It must have been four in the morning. In the still of night, the stars and the moon made everything . . . alive. We were arm in arm, and you had a funny look on your face. I said, "What's wrong?" And you said, "Nothing, I'm just happy." How can you just let go of that?

MIKE

I don't know. Sandy, the truth is I am thinking about leaving you.

SANDY

I know.

Lights cross to Frances.

FRANCES

And Mike did run from Sandy. Fast as he could. But there was one thing Mike couldn't run from.

Frances puts on a death mask.

Sound. Helicopter.

Dr. Chang and her Shadow dance on with two black chairs.

Mike and his Shadow sit.

Sound fades. A circle of light on Mike. We can see the dust floating from the heavens.

Wearing death masks, Chang's Shadow and Frances circle Mike.

DR. CHANG

Michael, I read about you in the *L.A. Times*. It said you're going to be working for a Congressman.

MIKE

Will I be alright?

DR. CHANG

Michael, this is why we need to look inside.

Music.

DR. CHANG'S SHADOW

Can you believe it? Five hundred dollars for a tune-up!

DR. CHANG

Normally, if a patient has your symptoms for two weeks, we don't worry. Even three. But Michael, I don't want you to worry. That is my job.

CHANG'S SHADOW

I know—I'll trade in for a new Mercedes.

DR. CHANG

We will take biopsies. A lab will give us a report. We'll know more once I look inside. It could be something so simple . . . like an ulcer.

MIKE

I'm scared.

MIKE'S SHADOW

I want to live.

DR. CHANG

Michael, I cannot promise. But do I think it's very possible whatever it is will be treatable. To some extent. I will see you at nine a.m.

Dr. Chang dances off. Mike dances with fear, trapped by the room.

MIKE'S SHADOW

I feel like Beckett. I can't go on. I must go on.

Blackout. Music. A light on Sandy. Mike dances to her.

SANDY

You startled me.

MIKE

I still have a key.

MIKE

I was in the hospital. Biopsies. I'll know soon.

SANDY

"I'm sorry, Mike. I need to be alone.

SANDY'S SHADOW

Go.

MIKE

Sandy . . . I may have can—

SANDY

(quickly) You're the one who ran from me.

Sandy's Shadow dances on with a large wind-up clock. It's ticking.

She slowly moves around the space in a circle, holding the ticking clock.

MIKE

Sandy, I don't have any idea if . . .

SANDY

Mike. I think you need to ask yourself why you're coming to me. You have other friends. I think . . . I think sometimes the people we care about the most . . . are not the people that are best for us. You ran—from me, everything. And now there's something you can't run from. I hope you're okay, Mike, but this time I'm going to run.

SANDY'S SHADOW

Time. Time. Time. *(pause)* Time.

SANDY

If the tests show a serious problem, call. Otherwise, goodbye, Michael.

Blackout.

Sound of wind.

Music through Speaker A.

Through Speaker B.

Baby crying.

Helicopter in the distance.

Lights up, slowly. Frances hovers over her grave. A narrow pathway of light leading to two Shadows in death masks, their backs to us.

They wear white T-shirts and stand on either side of a screen door, holding it.

Mike and his Shadow run in. Helicopter louder! Mike sees some writing on one of the shirts that we can't. He becomes very angry.

Helicopter louder! Mike pounds on screen door!

Helicopter as we've never heard it!!!

Mike makes a running start. Hits screen door. Shadows turn 180 degrees with Mike's impact, letting him through.

Sound out!

We immediately notice three things:

1. Mike is kneeling in the same position as on page one.

2. One of the Shadows' shirts reads, "Cemetery closed Saturdays." On the other Shadow's shirt, a Star of David.

3. Mike's Shadow is stuck on the other side of the screen door. He can only look in.

Mike is raw, alone.

MIKE

Mom?

Frances does not move.

MIKE

I feel your presence here . . . I was offered a job by a United States Congressman. I wanted to tell you. Every time a big event happens, I think about you. At your funeral, they gave us a little black ribbon to tear, which was to symbolize the tradition of tearing one's clothes. The ribbon looked like something mass produced for a gift card store.

Mike takes off jacket. Tears it. Slowly. Then, into shreds.

Worn. He sits.

MIKE

In the hospital . . .

Frances turns.

MIKE

They took biopsies. It could be nothing or it could be . . . Anyway, I wanted to tell you I'm sorry. That I've been running.

Mike cries. His face drops to his knees.

Frances steps down, Walks to screen door. Waves hand.

The screen door turns 180 degrees.

Mike's Shadow walks through the door.

Frances holds them both.

A moment. Very little light.

Still.

Darkness.

Lights up. Frances, alone, lights a candle.

FRANCES

It occurs to me even now, in telling this story, that if my parents had not run from Germany, I surely would never have been born. To run. Not to run. In the end, how are we to know? (*pause*) Well, it turned out Michael had only a small ulcer. He turned down the job with the Congressman—and ran after Sandy. Sandy ran for a while—until she didn't. Mike promised to visit me every year. (*shows flowers, smiles*) Look at what he brought me.

Dr. Chang's Shadow enters D.L., wearing white T-shirt, holding a white candle. She lights it.

Mike and Sandy's Shadows enter, CENTER, in white T-shirts, each with a candle. They light them.

Sandy and Mike enter, U.S. of their Shadows. She, with bridal veil; Mike, with tux tie. Each lights a white candle.

Dr. Chang enters U.C., as a female rabbi, to top off what is now a pyramid.

Rabbi places linen napkin with lightbulb under it in front of Mike. Lights candle.

FRANCES

(bittersweet) Life is a party. Make a wish!

Mike steps on napkin. Glass shatters! Frances blows out candle. The rest blow out candles.

END OF PLAY

CPSIA information can be obtained
at www.ICGtesting.com
Printed in the USA
LVOW12s1658270318
571328LV00003B/280/P